WORLD EXPLORERS

HERNANDO DE SOTO

Kristin Petrie

Checkerboard Library

An Imprint of Abdo Publishing
abdobooks.com

ABDOBOOKS.COM
Published by Abdo Publishing, a division of ABDO, PO Box 398166, Minneapolis, Minnesota 55439.

Printed in the United States of America, North Mankato, Minnesota
102021
012022

Design and Production: Tamara JM Peterson, Mighty Media, Inc.
Editor: Liz Salzmann
Cover Photograph: Prisma Archivo/Alamy Photo
Interior Photographs: Bettmann/Getty Images, p. 20; Byelikova_Oksana/iStockphoto, p. 17; Capt. S. Eastman/Library of Congress, pp. 21, 29 (top); Daniel Hernández Morillo/Wikimedia Commons, pp. 13, 28 (top); ESB Professional/Shutterstock Images, pp. 8–9; Grabado de Juan Brunetti por dibujo de José Maea/Wikimedia Commons, pp. 5, 28 (bottom); John Everett Millais/Wikimedia Commons, p. 15; John William Orr/Library of Congress, pp. 22–23; MicroOne/Shutterstock Images, pp. 18–19, 19 (inset map); Morphart Creation/Shutterstock Images, pp. 26–27, 29 (bottom); Songquan Deng/Shutterstock Images, p. 7; Titian/Wikimedia Commons, p. 11; traveler1116/iStockphoto, pp. 24–25; Wikimedia Commons, p. 6
Design Elements: Joseph Moxon/Flickr (map), Oleg Iatsun/Shutterstock Images (compass rose)

Library of Congress Control Number: 2021943037

Publisher's Cataloging-in-Publication Data
Names: Petrie, Kristin, author.
Title: Hernando de Soto / by Kristin Petrie
Description: Minneapolis, Minnesota : Abdo Publishing, 2022 | Series: World explorers | Includes online resources and index.
Identifiers: ISBN 9781532197307 (lib. bdg.) | ISBN 9781098219437 (ebook)
Subjects: LCSH: Soto, Hernando de, approximately 1500-1542--Juvenile literature. | Discovery and exploration--Juvenile literature. | Exploring expeditions--Juvenile literature. | Explorers--Biography--Juvenile literature.
Classification: DDC 970.01--dc23

CONTENTS

HERNANDO DE SOTO

Hernando de Soto lived during an **era** of exploration. His heroes were brave men who explored foreign lands. They returned to Spain with stories, gold, and respect. De Soto would do the same.

De Soto accomplished many things for Spain. He helped take over the Inca Empire. Later, he led expeditions throughout southern North America.

The Spanish government sent de Soto to establish Spanish colonies and convert the Native Americans to Christianity. De Soto's personal mission was to find gold and glory.

Hernando de Soto was determined and fearless. He helped conquer the New World for Spain. Unfortunately, greed and cruelty marked many Spanish explorations, including de Soto's. And Spain's growing empire caused the loss of the Native Americans' ways of life.

Hernando de Soto was a conquistador. Conquistadors were Spanish leaders and conquerors.

EARLY LIFE

Hernando de Soto was born in 1496 or 1497. His parents were Francisco Méndez de Soto and Leonor Arias Tinoco. They were minor **nobility**. Hernando had an older brother, Juan, and two sisters named Catalina and María. The de Soto family lived in Jerez de los Caballeros, a town in southwestern Spain.

Little is known about Hernando's early life. However, it is known that he could read and write. He also knew some Latin and mathematics. So, Hernando probably attended school or was tutored by local priests.

Hernando was influenced by stories of exploration and discovery. He heard about the travels of Spanish explorers such as Vasco Núñez de Balboa and Juan Ponce de León.

WOULD YOU?

Would you be inspired by explorers like Balboa and Ponce de León?

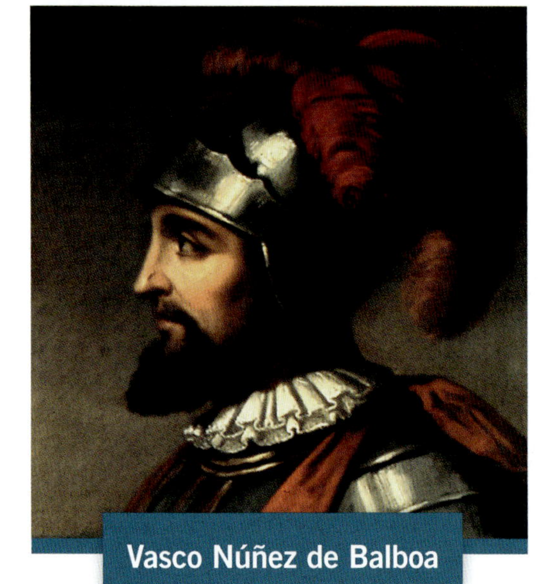

Vasco Núñez de Balboa

In 1513, Juan Ponce de León began his search for the mythical fountain of youth. During his search, he sailed to Florida.

FIRST TRAVELS

De Soto wanted to follow in the footsteps of other Spanish explorers. In 1514, he left his family and moved to Seville, Spain. He became a soldier under the command of Pedro Arias Dávila.

Arias Dávila was made governor of a new colony called Darién in Central America. De Soto sailed with him to the New World.

Native Americans in the New World had little defense against the Spaniards and their weapons. De Soto led his troops in raids against them. The Spaniards killed many Native Americans and enslaved others.

De Soto's reputation as a soldier and leader grew. And he was getting rich from his **conquests** of Native Americans. Soon, he was given more opportunities.

The old quarter of Seville, Spain

WEALTHY NATIONS

De Soto soon became involved in a new mission. In 1527, Spaniard Francisco Pizarro captured a number of Native Americans off the coast of South America. They were from the Inca Empire.

The Inca Empire was huge and powerful. It stretched more than 2,000 miles (3,200 km) down the west coast of South America. The empire extended into the Andes Mountains in the interior of the continent. Pizarro believed great wealth awaited him in this empire.

King Charles I of Spain granted Pizarro **permission** to attack the Inca Empire in 1529. De Soto then became involved in the **conquest**. He was already rich from other victories, so he lent Pizarro two ships.

WOULD YOU?

Would you want to join in the search for riches? What do you think you would look for?

King Charles I of Spain

THE INCAS

De Soto joined Pizarro and his army at Puná, in what is now Peru. De Soto brought additional men and horses. Because of his contributions, de Soto was made second in command.

As the army moved south through Peru, Pizarro and de Soto learned of a war taking place among the Incas. Five years earlier, the king of the Inca Empire had died. His two sons were fighting over who would rule the kingdom. This information pleased the Spaniards. Disagreement among the Incas would make it easier to conquer the empire.

In October, an Incan ambassador requested a peaceful meeting with the Spaniards. Pizarro agreed to meet with him. After exchanging gifts, the ambassador suggested the Spaniards continue on their journey. They would soon meet Atahualpa, one of the king's sons.

Francisco Pizarro on horseback. Pizarro's army included more than 50 horses. Having horses helped the Spaniards conquer the Incas.

AT CAJAMARCA

In early November, Pizarro and de Soto finally reached the Incan city of Cajamarca. There, they met the new Incan king Atahualpa. Atahualpa had an army of 30,000 warriors, while the Spanish army was down to 168 soldiers. Nevertheless, Pizarro formed a plan to take Atahualpa **hostage**.

To lure Atahualpa into his trap, Pizarro invited Atahualpa to a feast. Early on November 16, 1532, the Spanish soldiers hid in the abandoned buildings of Cajamarca. Later that day, the Incan king entered the city with an escort of unarmed Incas. The Spaniards attacked from all sides.

The battle lasted the rest of the day. About 7,000 Incas died and Atahualpa was captured. In the following weeks, the Incas collected a large **ransom** of gold and silver for their ruler's release. Pizarro took the ransom but killed Atahualpa anyway.

WOULD YOU?

Would you win a battle with 168 soldiers against 30,000 warriors? How do you think the Spaniards felt before the battle?

Pizarro's capture of Atahualpa

IN CHARGE

At the end of November 1533, the Spanish army took over the Incan capital of Cuzco. The next year, Pizarro named de Soto lieutenant governor of the city. De Soto returned to Spain in 1536. There, he married Isabel de Bobadilla. Isabel was the daughter of de Soto's past commander, Pedro Arias Dávila. The de Sotos lived in a luxurious home in Seville.

De Soto, however, was restless. Despite his successes, he'd always been second in command. He wanted to be in charge and to receive all the glory from a new **conquest**. He also wanted to find more treasure.

Spain's king, Charles I, sent de Soto to explore the land north of Cuba. It was called La Florida. On April 7, 1538, the expedition set sail from Spain. De Soto was in command of 10 ships, 700 men, and 250 horses.

WOULD YOU?

Would you want to be in charge of an expedition? What do you think de Soto said to convince King Charles I?

The ruins of Cuzco

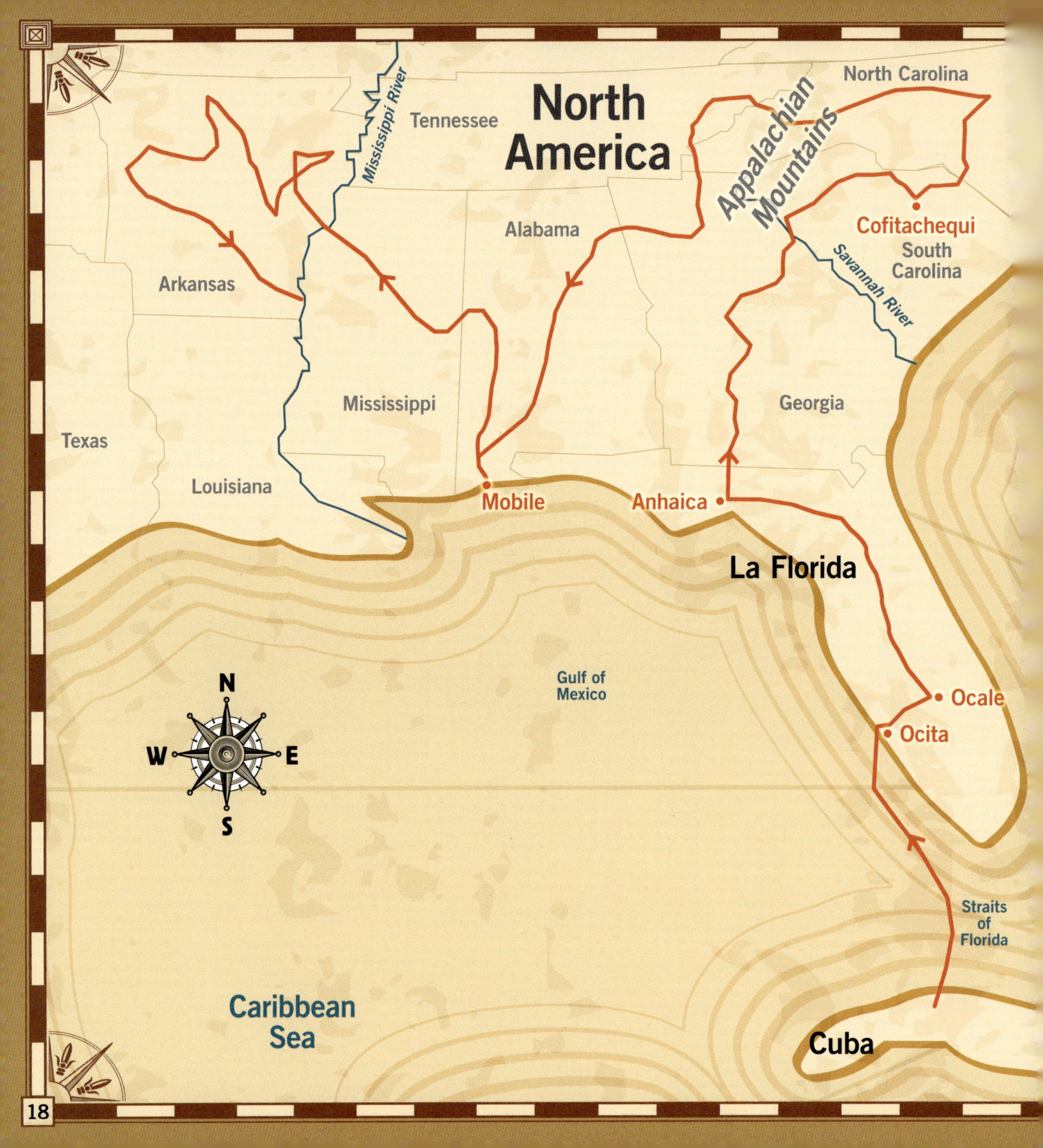
North America
Tennessee
Mississippi River
Appalachian Mountains
North Carolina
Arkansas
Alabama
Cofitachequi
South Carolina
Savannah River
Georgia
Mississippi
Texas
Louisiana
Mobile
Anhaica
La Florida
Gulf of Mexico
N
W
E
S
Ocale
Ocita
Straits of Florida
Caribbean Sea
Cuba

THE JOURNEY OF HERNANDO DE SOTO

1539 to 1542

Atlantic Ocean

LA FLORIDA

De Soto's **fleet** stopped at Cuba to prepare for the expedition. In May 1539, de Soto's crew sailed from Cuba to the shores of La Florida. There, they met a Spaniard named Juan Ortiz. In 1528, Ortiz had been separated from an earlier expedition. Since that time, he had lived with a Native American tribe. Ortiz became an interpreter for de Soto.

De Soto sent scouts in search of information about the region. They found no riches in the area. However, they heard rumors about a wealthy nation called Ocale to the northeast. De Soto led his soldiers to Ocale but found no gold.

However, the Spaniards stole the Native Americans' food and other supplies. To get rid of the **intruders**, the Native Americans told them another village to the north might contain gold.

Juan Ortiz being found by de Soto's crew

De Soto's fleet landed near present-day Tampa Bay.

COFITACHEQUI

De Soto reached the city of Anhaica in October 1539. He found no gold there, either. However, food was plentiful. De Soto and his army stayed there for the winter. Like the people in Ocale, the Anhaicans also told de Soto about other cities where he would find gold. The Native Americans had figured out how to get rid of the Spaniards.

In spring 1540, de Soto led his army north. The journey took them through present-day Georgia and South Carolina. On May 1, 1540, they reached the city of Cofitachequi.

The city's leader, the Lady of Cofitachequi, provided the army with food and housing. Her people gave the Spaniards pearls and copper. Many soldiers wanted to settle there, but de Soto pressed on. He believed gold and glory were still to be found.

The Lady of Cofitachequi greeted de Soto with pearls.

PUSHING ON

De Soto's expedition left Cofitachequi and headed west across the Appalachian Mountains. In October 1540, de Soto neared present-day Mobile, Alabama. There, thousands of Native Americans **ambushed** the Spaniards. In the battle, about 2,500 Native people died and de Soto claimed victory. But he had lost men, horses, and a lot of **ammunition** and food.

Still, de Soto pushed on. Over the next months, the expedition was attacked several more times. De Soto was victorious in these attacks as well. But he lost more men and horses. His remaining soldiers were injured and hungry. However, the relentless commander kept going west.

In May 1541, the expedition reached the Mississippi River. The soldiers built four large boats to carry them across the river. De Soto then led his men through present-day Arkansas.

De Soto was the first European to cross the Mississippi River.

LAST DAYS

In March 1542, de Soto decided to return to the Mississippi River. He planned to travel down the river to the Gulf of Mexico. There, he would establish a colony and send for **reinforcements**.

By the time the expedition reached the river, de Soto was very sick. He named Luis de Moscoso the new leader of the expedition. Hernando de Soto died on May 21, 1542.

With de Soto's death, the expedition ended. De Moscoso led the 311 remaining soldiers to Mexico. They arrived there in September 1543. De Soto is remembered for leading the march through today's southern United States. His expedition had accomplished much for Spain.

De Soto's soldiers buried his body in the Mississippi River.

TIMELINE

1514

De Soto sails to the New World with Pedro Arias Dávila.

1532

De Soto helps Francisco Pizarro attack the Inca Empire.

1496 or 1497

Hernando de Soto is born.

1533

De Soto and Pizarro take over Cuzco.

1539–1542

De Soto explores La Florida, the present-day southeastern United States.

1536

De Soto returns to Spain and marries Isabel de Bobadilla.

1542

Hernando de Soto dies on May 21.

GLOSSARY

ambush—to conduct a surprise attack from a hidden position.

ammunition—bullets, shells, and other items used in firearms.

conquest—the act of conquering.

era—a period of time or history.

fleet—a group of ships under one command.

hostage—a person held captive by another person or group who demands that certain things be done before the captured person will be freed.

intruder—a person who enters an area, such as another person's home, without permission.

nobility—the group of people who are members of the highest social class in some countries.

permission—formal consent.

ransom—money demanded for the release of a captive.

reinforcements—additional soldiers to strengthen an army.

SAYING IT

Appalachian—ah-puh-LAY-chuhn

Atahualpa—ah-tah-WAHL-pah

Cajamarca—kah-hah-MAHR-kah

Darién—dahr-YEHN

Jerez de los Caballeros—hay-REHTH day lohs kah-bah-YAY-rohs

Vasco Núñez de Balboa—VAHS-koh NOON-yayth day bahl-BOH-uh

ONLINE RESOURCES

To learn more about Hernando de Soto, please visit **abdobooklinks.com** or scan this QR code. These links are routinely monitored and updated to provide the most current information available.

INDEX